Preface

French for Kids 2 is a series of 3 course books. This is the second part for the earliest stage of learning French as a foreign language where students are able to understand some rules of their maternal language. This book is useful in the primary schools of India and abroad. This is intended to help the beginners and the parents to prepare their kids to start learning French as foreign language. This book provides a simple and interesting method of teaching to teachers and different ways of learning French to the students with an innovative approach.

This book should be of value as this book is integrated with pictorial representations for better visual learning experience for the kids. In this book, for the better understanding of our students every topic has different exercises for practice which can give confidence to the students.

At the end, I would like to say that the book is designed to equip both the teachers and the students with ideal guidance and exercises for practice.

Table of Contents

Lesson 1 (Leçon 1): Let's go to France (Allons en France)

Daughter: Papa, Where we are going?
Papa: My dear we are going to France.

Daughter: Papa, What we will see there?
Papa: My dear, we will see so many big cities in France, especially Paris, which is also known as "City of light". In Paris, we can visit the Eiffel Tower. It is the tallest monument over there.

Daughter: Papa, I am very excited to see the Eiffel Tower.

Papa: Nice is a city where we can see many parks like the Botanical Garden, Castle Hill Park, Parc Phoenix, Le Jardin Albert 1st, Jardin des Arènes de Cimiez, Parc Vigier, etc.

Daughter: Papa, I love parks, I hope it will be an interesting trip.

Papa: And you know, Marseille is the capital city of southern France. Marseille is known for its culture and cuisine, including the garlic and saffron flavored fish stew called Bouillabaisse.

À Vous

Exercise 1: Write down the names of cities from the map of France.

Exercise 2: Write down the names of parks of Nice.

Exercise 3: Fill the blanks.

1. ______________________ is a stew made up of garlic flavored fish.
2. Paris is also known as _________________________.
3. Capital city of southern France is _________________.
4. Tallest monument of France is __________________.
5. Bon Voyage means _____________________________.

Lesson 2 (Leçon 2) : Identify the marks on letters (Identifiez les marques sur les lettres.)

As you all have learnt alphabets in your previous class, in this book you will learn the use of alphabets in your day to day life.

For example:
How to write names?
How to write days of the months?
How to write your address?
How to write words using accents?

In this lesson, you will learn to use accents in French, so that you can make spellings.

Accents: These are small marks on the vowel letters. That can change the sound of the words and their meaning.

é This is the accent **aigu**. This accent can only be used on E.

Like
1. Télé – Television
2. Éléphant – Elephant
3. Bébé - Baby

At some places it changes the meaning of the word.

Like
1. Il mange - He is eating or He eats.
2. Il a mangé - He ate

À, à, È, è, Ù, ù

This is the accent **grave**. This accent works with letters **A, a, E, e, U, u**.

Like

1. Mère - Mother
2. Père - Father
3. Règle - Ruler

There is no difference in the sound of **ù** and **ù** or **à** and **à**. But both change the meaning of the word.

Like

1. Où – Where ; Ou - Or
2. Là – There ; La - The

â ê î ô û

This is the accent circonflexe. It does not change the sound of the letter but changes the meaning of the word.

Like

1. Mur - Wall Sur - On
2. Mûr - Mature Sûr - Sure

”

Ç=S

This is the accent cedilla or cédille. This accent works with the letter 'C' to show that you pronounce it like "s" rather than "k".

Like

1. Leçon - Lesson
2. Garçon - Boy
3. Français - French

ë/ï/ü

This is the accent **trema**. This accent works with **e, i, u**. The another name of this accent is umlaut. Putting two dots on the vowel breaks the word in two sounds.

Like

1. Noël - No + ël - Christmas
2. Maïs – Ma + ïs - Corn

LES ACCENTS FRANÇAIS

l' accent aigu	é	l' été un étranger
l' accent circonflexe	â ê î ô û	une âme une fenêtre une île l'hôtel août
l' accent grave	à è ù	là-bas très où
le tréma	ë ï ü	Noël un aï un capharnaüm
la cédille	ç	les garçons en français

À Vous

Exercise 1: With the help of above table put accents in the following words:

1. Garcon ____________
2. Tres ____________
3. Ile ____________
4. Mais ____________
5. Ou ____________
6. Mur ____________
7. Mere ____________
8. fenetre ____________

Lesson 3 (Leçon 3): What is the time? (Quelle heure est-il ?)

As you all have learnt numbers in your previous class, in this book, you will learn to use them in your day to day life.

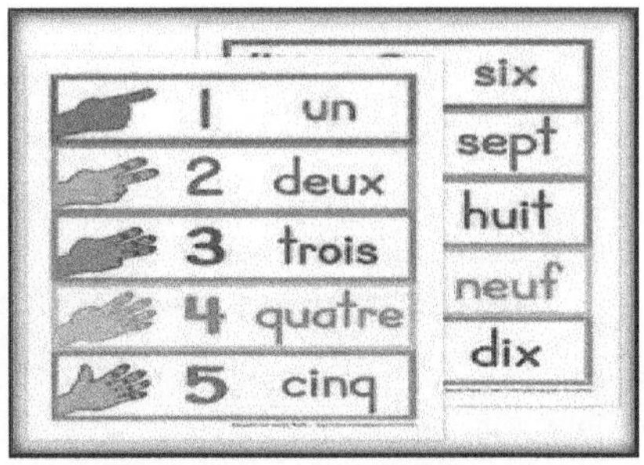

For example:
How much money do you have in your wallet?
How many days are there in a month?
What is your age?
What is the time now?

In this lesson, you will learn 'Telling time in French' so that you can prepare a daily routine.

Let's start
What is the time? (Quelle heure est-il ?)
To tell the time, it is necessary to use correct form of sentence.

It is …'O clock -- Il est……...heure/heures.

	It is 1'O clock.	Il est une heure.
	It is 2'O clock.	Il est deux heures.
	It is 3'O clock.	Il est trois heures.
	It is 4'O clock.	Il est quatre heures.

	It is 5'O clock.	Il est cinq heures.
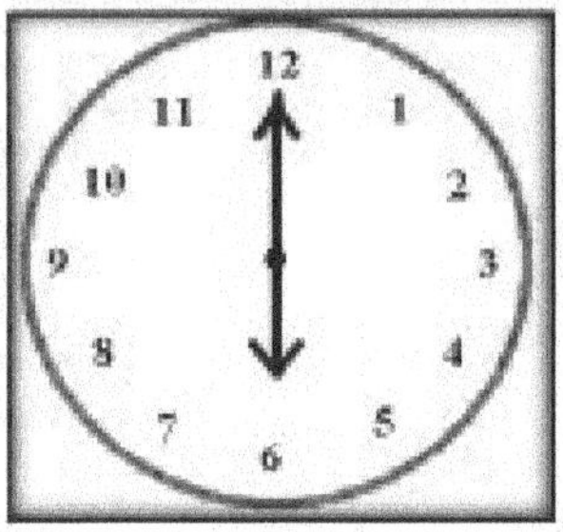	It is 6'O clock.	Il est six heures.
	It is 7'O clock.	Il est sept heures.
	It is 8'O clock.	Il est huit heures.

	It is 9'O clock.	Il est neuf heures.
	It is 10'O clock.	Il est dix heures.
	It is 11'O clock.	Il est onze heures.
	It is 12'O clock.	Il est douze heures.

To learn time, students must learn more cardinal numbers.
Cardinal numbers are simply numbers, which you are learning from pre-primary classes.

Let's Start-

11	Eleven	Onze
12	Twelve	Douze
13	Thirteen	Treize
14	Fourteen	Quatorze
15	Fifteen	Quinze
16	Sixteen	Seize
17	Seventeen	Dix-sept
18	Eighteen	Dix-huit
19	Nineteen	Dix-neuf
20	Twenty	Vingt

À Vous

Exercise 1: Write the following numbers in french:

1. 1 –

2. 2 –

3. 3 –

4. 4 –

5. 5 –

6. 6 –

7. 7 –

8. 8 –

9. 9 –

10. 10 –

11. 11 –

12. 12 –

13. 13 –

14. 14 –

15. 15 –

16. 16 –

17. 17 –

18. 18 –

19. 19 –

20. 20 –

Lesson 4 (Leçon4): Greetings (Salutations)

Dear students, every time when you meet someone, you use different words to greet them depending on who the person is. If it's your friend you use different greetings, but if it's someone older, you greet them differently.

Now you are going to learn these greetings in French.

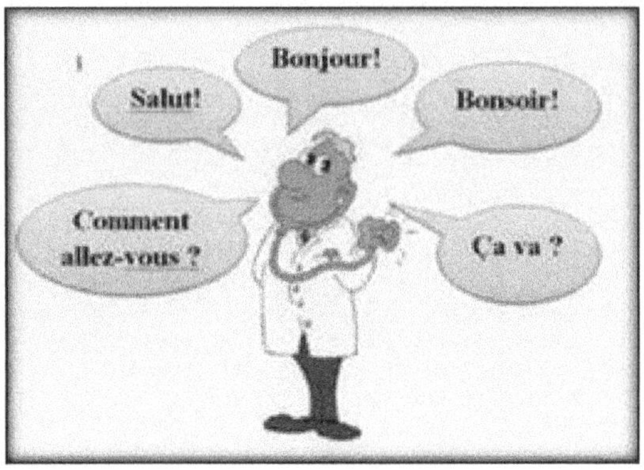

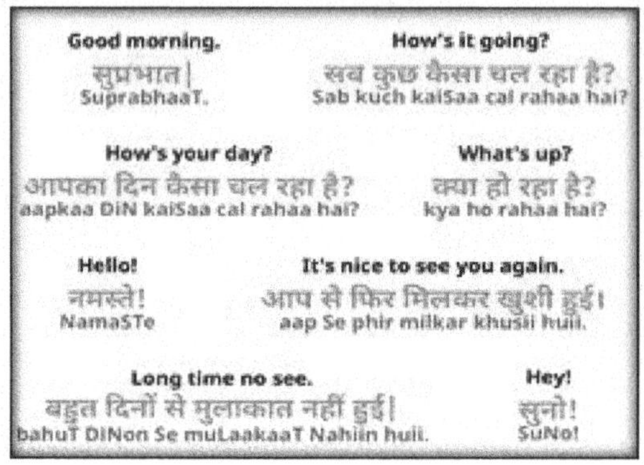

Now repeat again and again:

	Good morning / Good day	
Bonjour is a special word that we can use at any time of the day with anyone, be it an elder or a stranger. It means Good Morning, Hello or Good Day.		
	Good Afternoon	

Bon après-midi is a word which we can use only in afternoon and with anyone, be it an elder or a stranger.		
	Good evening	
Bonsoir is a word which we can use only in the evening after 6 pm and with anyone, be it an elder or a stranger.		
	Good night	
Bonne nuit is a word that we can use only at night, at the time of leaving anyone. After that here are some other greetings which we can use only with our friends.		
	Hi	
	Hi	
	Hi	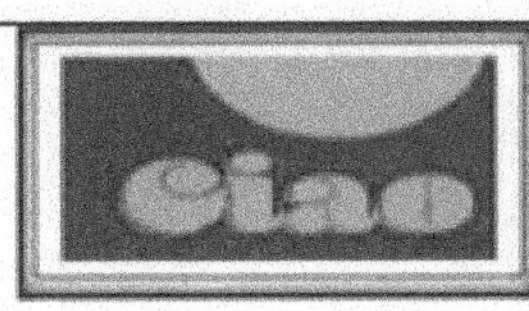

<table>
<tr><td></td><td>Nice to meet you.</td><td>
</td></tr>
<tr><td></td><td>Bye</td><td>
</td></tr>
<tr><td colspan="3">Like Bonne nuit, Au revoir is a word that we can use at the time of leaving anyone.
Leaving home, school, office or any place or person.</td></tr>
</table>

Whenever we greet anyone, there is a courtesy to ask **"How are you?"**
Now let's learn how to ask in French.

1. Comment ça va? - How are you?
2. Ça va super!- It's going great
3. Ça va très bien! - I am very fine.
4. Ça va bien! - I am fine.
5. Ça va, comme ci comme ça! - It's ok, so so .
6. Ça ne va pas! - I am not fine.
7. Ça va mal! - It's bad.
8. Ça va très mal ! - It's very bad.

À Vous

Exercise 1 : Fill the blanks with the help of correct words:

1. Bonne____________ !
2. _______________va !
3. Au ______________ !
4. Bon après_________ !
5. Ça va_________ mal !
6. Comme___comme __ !

Exercise 2 : Identify the image and put the correct word in the given blank.
(Bonsoir ; Comment ça va? ; Bonjour ; Au revoir ; Salut ; Ça va très mal ; Bon matin ; Bon après-midi)

____

____

____

Lesson 5 (Leçon 5): My name is Soni. And you, what's your name? (Je m'appelle Soni. Et toi, Comment tu t'appelles ?)

After learning greetings words and numbers, students are now able to introduce themselves by telling their name, their age, their place of living and some other describing words.

Two kids are in the garden for the plantation of their society. They want to be friends. Let's see, how they will start the interaction?

<table>
<tr><td colspan="3">Now, we will see how a formal conversation takes place in French.
This is the time of a new session, teacher wants to know her students like their names, their ages, and their places of living.</td></tr>
<tr><td>Bonjour les élèves !

Comment vous appelez-vous ?

Je m'appelle Divya.

Quel âge avez-vous ?

J'habite à Mohan Nagar.
Où habitez-vous?</td><td>
</td><td>Bonjour madame !

Je m'appelle Naman.

Je m'appelle Arjun .
Et vous madame ?
Comment vous appelez-vous ?

J'ai neuf ans.

J' ai 8 ans.</td></tr>
</table>

Au revoir !		Madame, où habitez-vous? J'habite à Rajendra Nagar. Au revoir madame !

Comment vous appelez-vous ?	What is your name ?
Je m'appelle……………..	My name is…………….
Quel âge avez-vous ?	What is your age?
J'ai …………….ans.	I am ……….years old.
Où habitez-vous?	Where do you live?
J'habite à…………….	I live in…………….

Note: Above sentences has to be used with elders and strangers or we can say Formally.

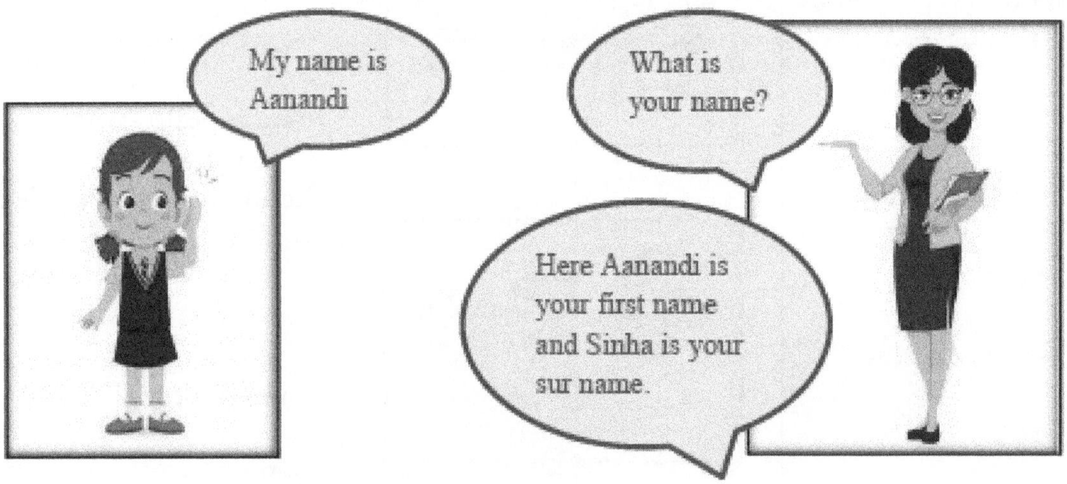

So, in French it is Prénom(first name) - Aanandi
Et(And)
Nom(Sur name) – Sinha

You can write just like this - Nom Prénom - Sinha Aanandi
This is also the correct form of telling name in France.

À Vous

Now write your name in two parts:
Nom:________________________;
Prénom:____________________________

Now write your father's name in two parts:
Nom:___________________________;
Prénom:___________________________

Now write your mother's name in two parts:
Nom:___________________________;
Prénom:___________________________

Now write your brother's name in two parts:
Nom:____________________________;
Prénom:__________________________

Now write your sister's name in two parts:
Nom:____________________________;
Prénom:__________________________

Lesson 6 (Leçon 6): I love my family (J'adore ma famille)

My name is Himesh. Today, come with me and meet my family. I live in a big family with my grandparents, parents, my uncle, my aunt, my cousins and my younger sister. Another member of my family is my pet dog.

Now, our teacher will tell us what do we say these relations in French.

	Mon grand-père Et Ma grand-mère	My grand father and My grand mother
	Mon oncle Et Ma tante	My uncle And My aunt
	Moi, Ma sœur Mon père Et Ma mère	Me My sister My father And My mother

	Mes cousins	My cousins
	Mon Chien	My dog

Points to remember: ***mon, ma, mes*** all words means ***My.***
We put them according to the number and gender of the noun.
Example: 1. Mother is singular and feminine so we use ma.
2. Father is singular and masculine so we use mon.
3. And with all plural nouns we use mes like in cousins.
In French we put adjectives according to the number and gender of the noun. In further classes you will learn these possessive adjectives.

I do so many different activities with my family members.

	Gardening	Le Jardinage
	Reading	La Lecture

	Celebration	La Fête
	Picnic	Le Pique-nique

Points to remember: Here, le and la means "the" in French. All the things in French also have gender so we put le/la before them according to their gender.

For feminine ……………… la

For masculine …………………….. le

À Vous

Exercise 1: Now you have to paste photos of your family members in the tree along with your pet (if any). Write their names in the given blanks:

1. ___________________________
2. ___________________________
3. ___________________________
4. ___________________________
5. ___________________________
6. ___________________________
7. ___________________________

8. ________________________________

9. ________________________________

Note: Students can draw more apples to paste photo if members are more than the given apples. Colour the apples red, if members are less than the given apples.

Lesson 7 (Leçon 7): Keep silence in the classroom (Gardez le silence dans la classe)

Today teacher is preparing the students prepare for craft activity. She wants to give some guidelines. Some students are creating noise. Let's see, how she is giving instructions:

Here are some instructions that teacher can give at the time of her class:
1. Taisez-vous ! (Shut your mouth!)
2. Asseyez-vous ! (Sit down!)
3. Écoutez attentivement ! (Listen attentively!)
4. Prenez votre papier ! (Take your paper!)
5. Coupez le papier ! (Cut the paper!)
6. Tenez les ciseaux !(Hold the scissors!)
7. Dessinez !(Draw!)
8. Gardez le silence !(Keep silence!)

9. Ne parlez pas !(Don't talk!)
10. Ne courez pas dans la classe !
11.(Don't run in the class!)
12. Écrivez proprement !(Write neatly!)
13. Faites attention !(Pay attention!)

These are some sentences that your teacher can use in the classroom or in the school bus.

Points to remember:

- Sentences are starting with the verbs.
- Sentences are ending with an Exclamation mark!

À Vous

Exercise 1: Look at the images carefully and fill the spaces by choosing the correct option.

Chantez bien ! (Sing well) ; Écoutez attentivement ! (Listen attentively) ; Lisez le livre !(Read the book) ; Montez sur l'arbre (climb on the tree) ; Ne touchez pas (Don't touch) ; Mangez des fruits (Eat some fruits).

 ______________________________

 ______________________________

 ______________________________

____

____

____

Lesson 8 (Leçon 8): I am growing every day, every month, every year.(Je grandis chaque jour, chaque mois, chaque année.)

Ayush was born on 4th January 2001 on Friday. After some days his grandmother said that her grandson is 14 days old. How is she calculating and mentioning the age?

She is calculating with the help of the day's name, i.e. Friday, names of the month, i.e. January, and the year, i.e. 2001. There are seven days in a week.
Look carefully: Week days in French are same as planets' name.

Les jours de la semaine (Week days)

1. Monday → lundi → from Lune (Moon)
2. Tuesday → mardi → from Mars (god/planet of war)
3. Wednesday → mercredi → from Mercure (Mercury)
4. Thursday → jeudi → from Jupiter (chief god/planet)
5. Friday → vendredi → from Vénus (Venus, goddess of love)
6. Saturday → samedi → from Saturne (Saturn)
7. Sunday → dimanche → from Dies Dominicus (Latin = "the Lord's Day")

After 5 weeks his grandmother said that now her grandson is a month old after January. There are 12 months in a year. Let's learn the months of the year in French.
Look carefully: Months' name in French.

Note: Week days' and months' names start with small letters in French.

Les mois de l'année (Month of the year)

1. janvier → january
2. février → february
3. mars → march
4. avril → april
5. mai → may
6. juin → june
7. juillet → july
8. août → august
9. septembre → september
10. octobre → october
11. novembre → november
12. décembre → december

À Vous

Exercise 1: Students will write their and their family members' name and birth dates in English and French both. Example is given for them:

Name	Date of Birth (English)	Date of Birth (French)
Ayush	4 January 2001	Le 4 janvier 2001

Note: French dates start by "Le".

Exercise 2: Fill the boxes

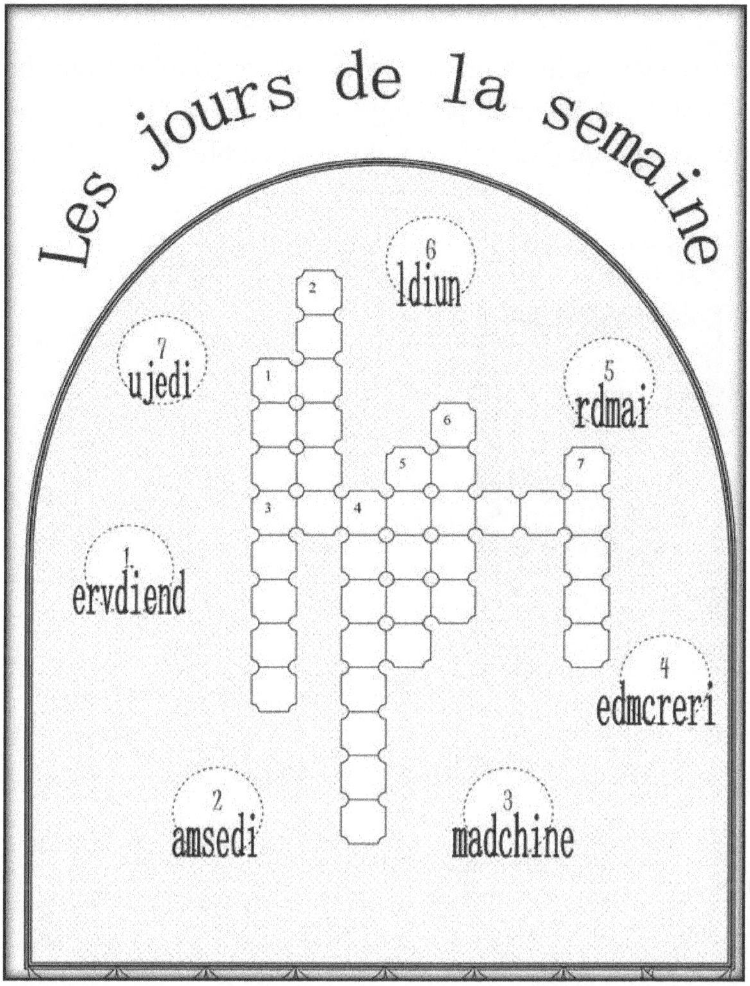

Lesson 9 (Leçon 9): How many questions ? (Combien de questions ?)

It is 2'O clock in the afternoon and Anant is leaving his home to buy some vegetables from the market. As he moved out of his house he saw a strange man passing by and suddenly a question arrived in his mind, "Who is this". He reached the market and went to a vegetable vendor. There he saw a type of vegetable that he had never seen before. He suddenly asked the vendor: What is this?" As he was returning home, he saw some strange animals walking along the street and again a question arrived in his mind, "What are these?"

Our mind creates these types of questions whenever we see something for the first time.
Now, let's learn how to ask such questions in French.

Who is this?	Qui est-ce?
This is Aryan	C'est Aryan.
For singular person	
What is this?	Qu'est-ce que c'est?
This is dog.	C'est un chien.
For singular animal	
What is this?	Qu'est-ce que c'est?
These are…	Ce sont…
For plural animals	
Who is this?	Qui est-ce?
These are….	Ce sont
For plural animals, persons	

One thing we should keep in mind here is that, in case of singular noun we will always respond by C'est and by Ce sont in case of plural nouns be it a person, animal, or thing.

À Vous

Exercise 1: Write the questions and answers by seeing the images.

 Un garçon	Q- ....
	A-...
 Des enfants	Q- ....
	A-...
 Des ballons	Q- ....
	A-...
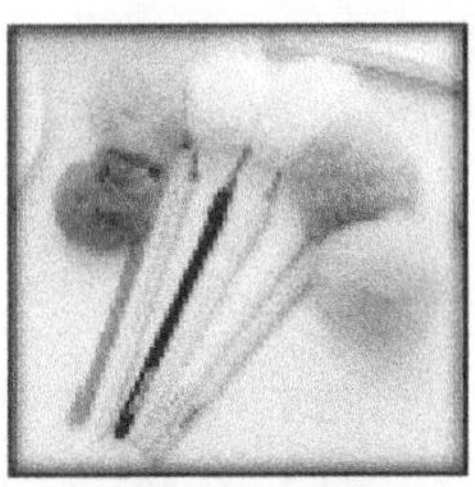 Des stylos	Q- ....
	A-...
 Des chocolats	Q- ....
	A-...

Lesson 10 (Leçon 10) : I have proud on my country (Je suis fier de mon pays)

After completion of the syllabus in school, students feel free, they want to play a game. The teacher allows them to discuss.

Tanvi : Ma'am, we can play ATLAS.

Julie ma'am : What is this game?

Tishya : Ma'am, in this game we need to write the country's names. We all say A, T, L, A, S then, I will write the name of country, starting with S like Spain. After me Alisha will write a country's name starting with the last letter of Sapin which is N.

Apoorv : Yes ma'am. If she will write Netherlands then again I will write a country's name starting with S other than Spain. I can write Switzerland.

Julie ma'am : That's a nice game.

A.T.L.A.S. - Spain - Netherlands - Switzerland - .....

Julie ma'am : I am happy to see that you all know the countries' name. Let's do it in French.

The country (Le pays)

India	Inde	

Germany	Allemagne	
France	France	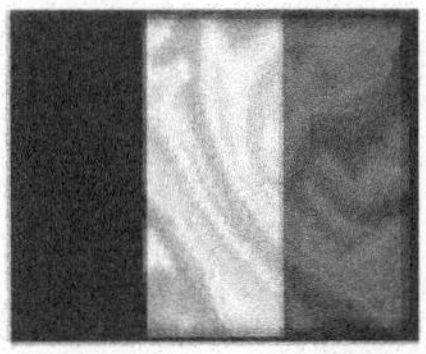
Switzerland	Swiss	
Spain	Espagne	
Netherlands	Pays bas	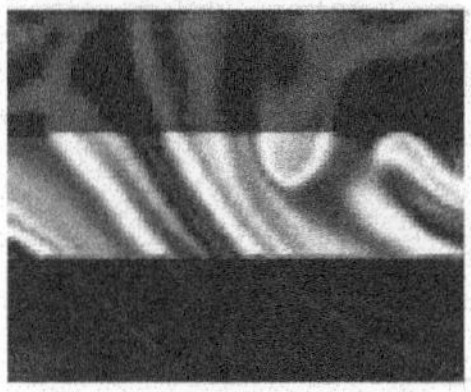

Note: The Netherlands and France are having same colors in their national flag but they are in different order.

Countries like all other nouns in French have gender, so we add, le/la/les before them which means "The" in English.

le-masculine, la-feminine, les-plural.

(l') put before the names starting with a vowel.

Nationality (Nationalité)

 India	Indien	 India	Indienne
 Canada	Canadien	 Canada	Canadienne
 Germany	Allemand	 Germany	Allemande
 France	Français	 France	Française
 Spain	Espagnol	 Spain	Espagnole

In French, nationalities also change according to the gender of the person which students have to learn carefully.

À Vous

Exercise 1: Find out the countries' names and write nationalities in the given space.

S	E	D	F	G	H	J	K	L	I
R	S	S	X	C	V	F	B	M	N
W	P	H	H	P	G	R	A	U	D
R	A	L	L	E	M	A	G	N	E
U	G	M	V	Q	A	N	D	G	K
O	N	J	U	I	O	C	S	A	X
P	E	I	M	N	C	E	S	D	H

Countries Name	**Nationalité**
______________	____________________
______________	____________________
______________	____________________
______________	____________________

À Vous

Answer (Réponses)

Leçon 1

Exercise 1: Nice, Lyon, Nantes, Marseille, Monpiller, Toulouse etc.

Exercise 2: Botanical garden, Castle Hill Park, Parc Phoenix, Le Jardin Albert 1er, Jardin des Arènes Cimiez, Parc Vigier, etc.

Exercise 3: 1. Bouillabaisse 2. City of light 3. Marseille 4. Eiffel tower 5. Happy journey

Leçon 2

Exercise 1:

1. Garçon
2. Très
3. île
4. Maïs
5. Où
6. Mûr
7. Mère
8. Fenêtre

Leçon 3

Exercise 1:

1. un
2. deux
3. trois
4. quatre
5. cinq
6. six
7. sept
8. huit
9. neuf
10. dix
11. onze
12. douze
13. treize

14. quatorze
15. quinze
16. seize
17. dix-sept
18. dix-huit
19. dix-neuf
20. vingt

Leçon 4

Exercise 1:
1. nuit
2. Ça
3. revoir
4. midi
5. très
6. ci, ça

Exercise 2 :

	_____ Bon matin___		______ Bonjour ___
	_ Comment ça va?___		______ Bonsoir ___
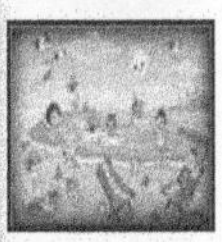	___ Bon après-midi_		_____ Au revoir ___
	__ Ça va très mal ___		_______ Salut _____

Leçon 5

Exercise 1: Answer can vary as per student's family.

Leçon 6

Exercise 1: Answer can vary as per student's choice.

Leçon 7

Exercise 1:

	Lisez le livre !
	Ne touchez pas !
	Mangez des fruits !
	Montez sur l'arbre
	Chantez bien !
	Écoutez attentivement !

Leçon 8

Exercise 1: Answer can vary as per student's family members.

Exercise 2:

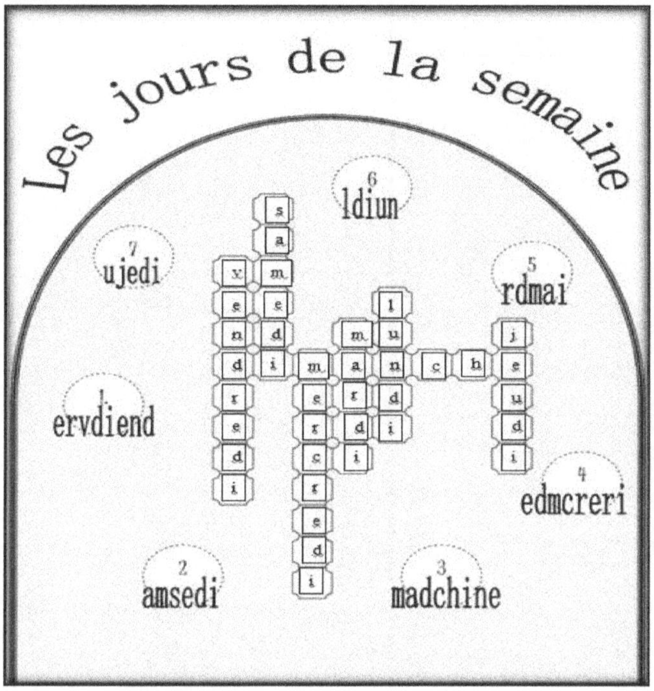

Leçon 9

Exercise 1:

 un garçon	Q- ....Qui est - ce ?............... A-..............C'est un garçon, ...
 des enfants	Q- ....Qui est- ce ?.............. A-...........Ce sont des enfants..............
 des ballons	Q- ....Qu'est-ce que c'est ?......... A-..........Ce sont des ballons.............
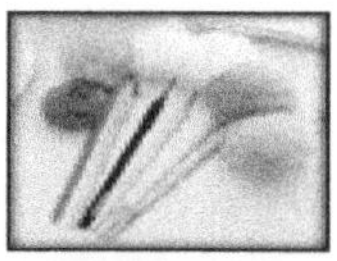 des stylos	Q- .... Qu'est-ce que c'est ?.......... A-.......... Ce sont des stylos.............
 des chocolats	Q- ....Qu'est-ce que c'est ?............ A-...... Ce sont des stylos ....

Leçon 10

Exercise 1:

S	E	D	F	G	H	J	K	L	I
R	S	S	X	C	V	F	B	M	N
W	P	H	H	P	G	R	A	U	D
R	A	L	L	E	M	A	G	N	E
U	G	M	V	Q	A	N	D	G	K
O	N	J	U	I	O	C	S	A	X
P	E	I	M	N	C	E	S	D	H

Français ; Indien ; Allemand ; Espagnol

9 789369 916993

Printed at Repro India Ltd.